Weaponized People:

Trump's Eurasian Army of Trolls

--by Laurel Federbush

C 2017

[Note: I got started on researching the subjects of this book from two different things that turned out to be related. One was a suspicion that certain religious leaders might be indoctrinating their congregations to see Donald Trump as some kind of holy man or messiah, since so many of his supporters apparently do (and no one else does). It turned out that, at least for one particular set of his supporters, the relevant factor wasn't churches at all but, rather, computer memes. The other area of research began as a result of my horror when a (former) Facebook friend approvingly posted a neo-Nazi video (of Lana Lotkeff of the Swedish hate megaphone Red Ice Radio, it turns out) in the comments section for one of my posts. I started looking into the creepy groups involved with the video, their groups and associates, and in my readings I twice came upon references to some Eurasian land bridge...]

All aboard the Trump Train!

For those of you who might not know, that's a meme, or recurring computer image, put out by the Trump campaign. A train that is, to use their word, "unstoppable."

Where is the Trump Train taking us? One thing many of his supporters cheer him on for is his anti-globalist populism. No "New World Order" on his watch!

In another part of the world, there's something else that was recently symbolized by a train.

The Eurasia Friendship Express 2015, was a joint venture between Russia and South Korea, and sought to strengthen relations between the countries of Eurasia. Some claim that the Eurasian Century is "unstoppable."

Trump...an unstoppable train...Eurasia...

You've heard of Eurasia, haven't you?

George Orwell had it as one of the three superstates in his dystopian novel <u>1984</u>. But it isn't just fiction.

You've probably heard of the New World Order. All the elites in their secret societies since time immemorial conspiring for world domination to enslave humankind. —Wait, "mankind." Political correctness is part of their conspiracy.

So on one side, there's the New World Order, embodied by the globalists of the world and their various organizations. On the other side, a random assortment of patriotic and nationalist movements, and those who are simply individualists or libertarian-minded, not wanting anyone to tell them what to do.

Nationalist movements all over the world, sometimes winning elections or referendums. Brexit, for example. Putting up a pretty good fight in France.

Lots of independent movements, simply seeking to preserve their own sovereignty against the globalist threat. Right?

No, alt-right.

They're creeping out from under the shadows. Haven't you seen them? The hate groups. The KKK, the Nazis, and their ilk. Once outcasts, now being welcomed into the mainstream. They've taken over one of the two major political parties of the United States. Even our president assures us that some of them are very fine people. The alt-right.

Where there is a conspiracy, there is likely to be a counter-conspiracy, especially where the stakes are as high as world domination.

Enter the Eurasianists.

Back in the 19th century, Madame Helena Blavatsky, the occultist founder of the Theosophical Society, talked about uniting the countries of Central Asia to create a superpower to counter the British Empire, of which the United States has assumed the mantle. She may be about to get her wish.

First, a bit about geography.

The idea of Eurasia being one big continent is hardly new, and the idea that the countries there might want to unify might not seem like a remarkable development. Russia already has territory in both continents. But it's a little more expansive than that.

As you might have guessed from the name, it's basically about uniting the countries of Europe and Asia to become the world's dominant continent. Russia is by far the most powerful, but it's pretty good for China, too.

According to the Eurasianists' plan, the world will be divided into a few "great spaces," and "geo-economic belts." There's the Euro-African Belt, the Asian-Pacific Belt, the Eurasian Continental Belt, and the American Belt. See that American one? Yep, they have plans for us.

They say they want a multipolar world, as opposed to the current unipolar one run by the United States. They want it to be network-centric (being part of a complex community). So you'd get the feeling it's kind of a freeform place, with lots of different regions sharing power.

Wrong. They also say they want Russia to be the nucleus, the strategic power center of a rigid hierarchical structure. So all parts of Eurasia are equal, but some are more equal than others.

So there's this Eurasian land bridge, and they want to unite it, by sea routes and by railroads.

Lyndon LaRouche and his Schiller Institute even favor a "World Landbridge," for greater prosperity for everyone, the current system being so "unjust."

Some of the economic initiatives and groups helping with land-bridgeness:

China's "One Belt, One Road" (OBOR), sometimes called the New Silk Road, an infrastructure program of roads, bridges, ports, railways, gas pipelines, etc., across more than 60 countries, land and sea. Oddly, the United Nations, which one would assume would be the bastion of globalism, generally supports this initiative. When Donald Trump turned his back on the Trans-Pacific Partnership, he gave OBOR a huge boost—and helped Eurasianism.

The Eurasian Economic Union, ratified in 2004, and made up of Belarus, Kazakhstan, Russia, Kyrgyzstan, and Tajikistan. It has its own currency, the altyn, backed by gold. To make the U.S. dollar useless. Also, having fiat currency, as we do in the west, helps ensure, among other things, that international agreements will be enforced. The gold standard allows countries to ignore them, so it is much more difficult for the international community to punish a bad-acting member country. So they are immunizing themselves against any sanctions that NATO countries may want to impose against them in the future.

BRICS, an association of Brazil, Russia, India, China, and South Africa, trading in their own currencies to get away from the U.S. dollar.

The Shanghai Cooperation Association, giving rise to the Russian-Chinese Strategic Partnership.

What kind of world would we have under Eurasianism?

Let's mention here that Steve Bannon, one of President Trump's principal advisors, whether in or out of the administration, gave a talk inside the Vatican in 2014 in which he mentioned "Eurasianism" and in the next breath praised Vladimir Putin as a champion of traditionalism and nationalism. So the man who is arguably "Trump's Brain" would seem to be a fan.

The man known as "Putin's Brain," on the other hand, is Russian philosopher Alexander Dugin, author of the book <u>The Fourth Political Theory</u> (the first three being liberal democracy, Marxism, and fascism). He has advocated for a "fascist fascism"--as if there were any other variety.

The book has been called "evil" and "allegedly conservative but actually neo-pagan" by the National Review, and its philosophy, Eurasianism, a "satanic cult."

Think of those programs you can sometimes find on the History Channel about the strange occult beliefs of the Nazis. Eurasianism is built upon those beliefs.

In Dugin's worldview, the concept of individual rights is a bad thing because it's imposed from the west. Same with modernity and advancement.

He says we should put aside our bias against fascism, and should embrace chaos.

Authoritarianism is a good thing. Also, he wants to bring about the end of the world.

Richard Spencer, alt-right founder of the National Policy Institute, loves Dugin's ideas and has been spreading them. "Alt-right," short for "alternative-right," is basically a trendy new term for white supremacist.

Check out "Eurasia Above All: the Manifesto of the Eurasist Movement" where it assures us that its goal is anything but a liberal democracy.

Eurasia happens to be the birthplace of the Aryan race, according to pseudoscientists, at any rate. That tidbit keeps coming up in Eurasianist writings, a propos of nothing. I wonder why...

Despite the fact that the manifesto mentions "the Jew" as being among those welcome, and "The Ideological Platform of the Eurasian Movement" stresses the belief that no ethnic group is superior or inferior and that eugenics is wrong, the Eurasian Movement is virulently anti-Semitic, transparently using hatred for the Jews as a way to unite different factions against a common "enemy," or bogey man.

Eurasianists sometimes refer to Americans and globalists as "Atlanticists," or sea-based people, as opposed to themselves, the land-based people. The sea-based people depend upon commerce...which means, of course, that they are riddled with Jews. The land-based Russians, they assure us, have been Aryan since the prehistoric times. The symbol on the Eurasian flag, a wheel of eight equally-spaced arrows emerging in different directions from a single point, identified by many as a symbol of chaos (something Dugin likes) and by me as a symbol of expansionism, is eerily reminiscent of a swastika.

The Eurasianists (sometimes called neo-Eurasianists) present themselves as the guardians of traditional Christian values, except for when they're pandering to the anti-Semitic neo-pagans, who despise Judeo-Christian civilization.

The patriarchy is necessary for every aspect of Eurasian life, and heterosexual marriage the unit upon which their society is built.

And...racially segregated ethno-states are fine and dandy. Especially the white ones. That may not be in the Eurasianists' official writings, but it is in the urgings of many of its chief advocates. And Dugin, father of the Eurasian Movement, praises white nationalists' traditionalism if not all of their actions, and urges identitarians who seek their own ethno-states to get on board with Eurasianism.

White ethnocentric nationalists, such as those who would like the United States to become a white ethno-state, have bought into Eurasianism. Proving once again (as if it needed proving) that they aren't very bright. Because if you're a nationalist, white ethnocentric or other, why would you trust a mega-state like Eurasia to uphold your borders or your traditional ethnic integrity? Have China and Russia proven to be good stewards of such things in the past?

Or maybe the white ethnocentric nationalists have thought of that but just don't care. Maybe they're willing to risk long-term pain for short-term support from Russia and wealthy Eurasianists who think they're anti-globalists.

Without the white ethnocentric part, we might rightly sympathize with some nationalistic aspirations. Perhaps we have them ourselves. And certainly not everyone in favor of the Eurasian concept is a white nationalist, or a racist of any kind. The writings put forward by the Eurasianist Movement are deliberately deceptive, making themselves appear the epitome of tolerance if you don't look too closely.

By the way, not everyone who talks about Eurasia or has "Eurasia" in the name of their organization is a Eurasianist. The group or individual in question may just be dealing with that part of the world. But it's the Eurasianists and the Eurasianist Movement, or the Eurasian Movement, who are the ones advocating this world dominance thing. You'd need to look into the beliefs and aims of a specific entity to know if it's in the Eurasianist camp or not.

Perhaps we fear the New World Order. Perhaps we see globalists trampling upon the oppressed peoples of the world.

But I'm siding with the globalists in this, and I don't even believe the earth is a globe. I think it's flat. But that's another matter.

Let me point out something that may not be obvious to everyone. At least I didn't know it when I started writing this. The New World Order and globalism aren't the same thing.

The New World Order is...who knows? It's supposedly the aim toward which the secret societies are conspiring, and they haven't told us

what it is. A one-world government of some kind
is the general assumption about what it is.

Globalism, however, is not a secret doctrine.
People go around being proud to be "global
citizens." Globalism, simply, is being aware of
how our world is interconnected. It's for
democracy, against empires, and for multicultural
decision-making about world matters. And you
keep your country, state, and local government.

About that "New World Order." I'm not a
freemason, and haven't been initiated into any
secret societies. Except a music fraternity, and I
don't think that really counts. But if you study any
of the alarmist books about the New World Order,
you will soon find that an inordinate number of
those who have made major, beneficial
contributions to our politics, religion, culture, or
science are members of at least one of the secret
societies alleged to be promoting the New World
Order. The Founding Fathers of the United States
included freemasons, and just look at all the New
World Order symbolism on our currency. It's even
been proposed that the United States was
founded specifically to further the New World

Order's aims. That's what the New World Order alarmists are saying, not its propagandists.

Well, if the New World Order gave us the United States of America, then I hardly think it's something American patriots should be hostile towards.

Not that globalism is necessarily aligned with the New World Order—I don't know if it is. But even if so, that's clearly the side on which you'll find the American ideals that are the foundation of our country.

In other words: if you're an American nationalist, believe it or not, you need to be a globalist.

Actually, in some of Eurasianist the writings, the words "globalist" and "western" are interchangeable. So the fight against globalism is really a fight against western values.

When the Eurasianists say "western," what they mean is American or supportive of America. So that's how the word is used in this book. The Eurasianists are, by definition, anti-American. Anti-globalists are all their pawns if not their accomplices.

The Eurasianists want to unite the whole non-western world against the west. So it isn't just that Russia could rival us on the world stage, or maybe China, or Iran could be a threat. It's ALL THE OTHER COUNTRIES TOGETHER against the United States and our allies.

It's a zero-sum game. Whatever hurts the globalists helps the Eurasianists, and vice versa.

There is going to be a world order, of one kind or another. Either we can go with the globalists and have one based on cooperation, tolerance, and sharing; or we can have the Eurasianists' world of genocidal racialism. Gee, that's a tough one, isn't it?

Now, the Eurasianists' goal may actually be unrealistic. The countries they would like to unite against the west all have their own agendas which are often at odds with each other. These conflicts and the resulting animus towards each other might be more relevant to some than any desire to destroy American influence. It's hard for me to see how this huge Eurasian alliance would hold together, with so much internal dissension. It might not last long enough to actually do us any harm. But if others are calling it "unstoppable," and the initiatives to build up Eurasia are already in place, then we need to take this very seriously.

The Eurasianists are a clear and present danger to us, but this is virtually never reported to us. Why not? Because it would sound like hysteria? Because discussing the Eurasian conspiracy would force the powers-that-be to admit to their own New World Order conspiracy?   But globalism has the potential to be beneficial to us all, and in so many ways it already is.

Here's today's choice: you can be a globalist or a Eurasianist. Notice I didn't say "anti-globalist." Because that ends up being the same as being a Eurasianist.

If you care about any of the ideals of western civilization—freedom, equal rights, self-government--however poor a job of living up to them the actual western civilization may have done, you have to side with the globalists. Because those certainly aren't Russian values, and they aren't Chinese values. So they won't be Eurasian values. Oh, did I mention that another major player in the Eurasian scheme is Iran, that bastion of human rights?

The world is like the United States' two-party system. It's a binary choice. You can have one or the other. Third-party options just help one or the other of the two real sides.

The United States (until Trump, at least) and its allies have been major players on the globalist stage. Not the only players, otherwise it would be imperialism. And maybe the roles they play or the lines they speak aren't always what we think they should be. That's when we can try, through democratic means, to steer things in a different direction. But if we want to remain free—and we surely do--we ought to always keep in mind the objective of keeping the United States and its allies, and its alliances, pre-eminent in the world.

The North Atlantic Treaty Organization (NATO) and the European Union (EU) are two alliances crucial to globalism, and lately under attack by Trump and other "populists."

This is the place where the far-left and far-right meet: trying to take down America and the west.

We need America. Therefore, we need to support globalism.

-"But I'm pro-life." So am I. And globalists have been pretty poor so far on this issue. But do you think that the unborn will be better protected by "one-child" China? The more extreme racist elements being energized by the Eurasianists openly believe in abortion for the undesirable races. And, needless to say, countless unborn babies are killed when there's genocide, which is what these racists advocate. Bringing down western civilization is no way to support life. Reasoned debate within a free global society is the only way we can, eventually, win.

-"We can't be the world's policeman." But we have to be. Who will do it better? The policeman (or policewoman) analogy is a good one. What would happen if all the good cops just quit? Or if there were no police? Could your life just go on peacefully as usual? You know the answer to that. If China and Russia become the world's policemen, do you think we'd be able to remain safe within our borders? Weakness is provocative, as they say. And so is isolationism.

-"Okay, but where's the threat? It's not as if Eurasia is about to attack us."

Actually, we are already under attack.

Russia's successful cyber warfare campaign to influence our election. They gave us President Trump.

As simultaneously silly and evil as Donald Trump may be, one aspect of Russia's cyber warfare campaign may be even more so.

Ever heard of Pepe the Frog?

Perhaps you know him as a cool and trendy internet meme, of innocent origins but co-opted by the alt-right as a symbol of racism and hate. But wasn't it funny when Hillary Clinton and her supporters over-reacted to a cartoon frog?

Have you ever wondered why Pepe is so ubiquitous? How has the symbol caught on so much?

Beyond the fact that he may be kind of cute, and have a certain attitude, there's another aspect of Pepe's rise that many people may not be aware of. But many are.

Through a bizarre set of the most unbelievable coincidences that I won't even try to explain, not being a techie myself, people who frequent the political internet message boards of 4chan and Reddit have come to believe that Pepe is actually an avatar of the Egyptian frog-deity Kek, god of chaos (chaos again!), and that Donald Trump is his human embodiment. It involves numerology, and a variant of chaos magic (and again...) called "meme magic," which—you'll never guess!--is the idea that memes are actually magic.

Except...well, that's bullshit.

Not to internet trolls, though. This is their religion.

What the internet people would say, of course, is that they don't really believe in this supposed Pepe/Kek god, that it's all one big joke, they know Trump isn't really a god, that those of us who get all riled up about Pepe are just uptight "normies" (people not in on their jokes), etc., etc.

But these are people who spend their lives on the internet, living in a simulated world. Their internet reality is more real to them than the real world.

Maybe they do know there's some difference between simulation and reality, since they get excited by the idea that their online activity could have real-world consequences—and the irony is that the way they could exercise even more power in the real world is by getting off the damn computer and doing something real. (I say, as I use a computer to write this.)

But their concept of what's real and what's not real, what's a joke and what's serious, isn't the same as it is to us "normies." What's not real may be even more "real" to them than what actually is. It's certainly more meaningful.

The fact that it isn't supposed to be real makes it, in a way, more dangerous. People tend to be more receptive to something that isn't supposed to be serious or real. Why guard yourself against a cartoon? Religious evangelists, in fact, might have more success sometimes if they wouldn't be so serious. They could say the Jesus thing is all one big joke. They wouldn't say that, of course. But people without principle would say or imply such a thing about what they're selling, especially if they know it's bunk.

For all intents and purposes, Pepe/Kek/Trump is actually their god. When you see that goofy image of a silly green cartoon frog, realize that you're looking at a cult deity.

And they have other proof, unrelated to Pepe or Trump, that meme magic is real. For example, someone in their forum predicts a celebrity's death, and lo and behold, that celebrity dies.

They wished for an incredibly bitter winter to curb the flow of immigrants, and got their wish that refugees would freeze and die.

Pernicious racists that they are, they once united to troll Africans not to trust the medical community, and then rejoiced when Ebola spread. Now I don't see how that can be attributed to magic, since it involved actual actions, but it gets included in their sick litany of purported miracles.

Meme magic!

Bullshit.

I would submit that anyone who is promoting this idea that meme magic is real and Trump is linked to Pepe/Kek is either very gullible, or else they're in on the conspiracy.

So who is it that is promoting this nonsense?

-Richard Spencer, who is the most obvious link between Eurasianism (fan of Dugin, remember?) and the cult of Pepe memes. Spencer is president of the white "identitarian" (sounds better than white supremacist, doesn't it?) National Policy Institute, who came up with the term "alt/right" to begin with. You may remember that Spencer is a disciple of Eurasianist philosopher Alexander Dugin. You may also be familiar with his "Hail Trump!"/Nazi salute video. Anyway, Spencer once tweeted, "Can Kek, meme magic and Russian hackers help me win election to Congress?" I wouldn't bet on the first two, but the last one maybe...and make that Eurasianist hackers. "Russia" is too limiting.

You can see this, too, on YouTube video: giving an interview at Trump's inauguration, Spencer points to his green pin, starts explaining about Pepe, and then gets punched by masked "protester."

Playing on the reputation of Kek as the Egyptian god of chaos. Yes, it's a theme with these folks. Remember how Spencer's guru, Alexander Dugin, father of the Eurasianist movement, thought chaos was cool? Why not promote the idea? In fact, reports are that Spencer was actually punched two different times that day. Guess they had to practice to get it right.

Incidentally, I suspect the leftist group Antifa of being in league with the alt-right groups it organizes violent protests against. Either they may be deliberately working together for maximum publicity for each, or else they get their instructions from the same source.

-Former Trump adviser Steve Bannon, who threatened that "Pepe's gonna stomp their ass," meaning he would rally his infamous Breitbart site's troll army when Paul Ryan seemed inclined to deny Trump the party's nomination.

Andrew Breitbart, I believe, was a decent and ethical if controversial man whose premature death is regrettable. If there were possibly any foul play, although that has been denied by every reputable source, I would look not to the left for possible enemies but to the alt-right (no individual is to be suspected, that's just the general direction), for whom the Breitbart News Network he founded was deliberately made into a platform upon his death.

-The now-domainless, former neo-Nazi website The Daily Stormer, whose associate, the convicted internet hacker Andrew Auernheimer (a.k.a. "Weev") bragged about having trained an army of thousands of trolls to subject certain reporters and Hillary Clinton staff people to relentless harassment for about a year using Pepe images simulating rape and necrophilia, among other forms of harassment; making Ms. Clinton look silly when she publicly complained about a cartoon frog. Auernheimer said he liked using Pepe because the frog imagery was reminiscent of the Biblical plague of frogs. Nice to know he draws inspiration from the Bible.

That troll army of The Daily Stormer—real nice bunch of folks. They were also credited with threatening CNN staffers after they outed one of these trolls for a video he made and posted, simulating Trump pummeling a wrestler whose face was covered by the CNN logo.

The Daily Stormer's founder, Andrew Anglin, led his troll army on another noble mission: terrorizing a Jewish woman, her husband, and 12-year-old son with hundreds of death threats and Holocaust references. The woman had urged the mother of our friend Richard Spencer to renounce her son's white supremacist views, which for some reason had been getting bad publicity, so that the small Montana town they shared could have some peace. Anglin threatened also to organize a Nazi march (which, thank God, never materialized) through the town, home of many Holocaust survivors.

Following the Charlottesville "Unite the Right" KKK/neo-Nazi rally that it had helped organize and that resulted in the death of a woman protesting the hate groups, The Daily Stormer was booted off its website. It promptly set up another one in Russia (!) after being refused by US internet domains—but the Russian domain almost immediately booted them off, too. Russia's media watchdog complained that the site violated their laws against hate speech. Proving, thereby, that there are good, moral people everywhere, in Russia as well as any other place, despite what Putin and his cronies may be cooking up.

Anyway, you'll notice that Breitbart has a troll army, and the neo-Nazi website The Daily Stormer has a troll army. Would those be completely different people, or might some of them overlap? Perhaps a lot of them? And would it be a problem if an advisor to the president is marshaling neo-Nazi trolls, and at least threatened to use them to help him get into office? It doesn't really matter much if Bannon denounces the white ethnocentrists, as he has of late. He has deliberately given Spencer's alt-right a platform and continues to rally its racist goons to his—and Trump's—cause.

It may be noted that similar harassment to the cases here has been reported in Finland, experienced by a journalist as she tried to report on the existence of the virulently pro-Russian troll armies.

Back to the Pepe hoaxers:

-Donald Trump, Jr. posted a picture on Instagram called "The Deplorables," showing his father, President Trump, standing right next to Pepe, along with other of his more prominent supporters. Pepe is the only one who's a cartoon, unless you count Donald Trump...

-President Trump himself. People say that Trump is reluctant to alienate the racists of the alt-right because they're his base. That's not the whole picture. He doesn't see them as a voting bloc. He sees them as his troops, and rightly so--they are. Trump as a candidate in 2016 did a Q&A session for The_Donald, a major pro-Trump reddit forum that's a major site of Pepe and troll activity). Since he has become president, there have been numerous posts in this forum about "meme warfare," a category of cyber warfare that the CIA has actually set up a unit to address. The_Donald's folks brag that they've waged war against the CIA and won. Why is a pro-Trump site that the man himself has honored with a visit waging a cyber war against the CIA?

And did you notice the weird and silly faces that Trump kept making during his debates with Hillary

Clinton? Of course you did—they went on for several seconds, just to make sure no one could miss them. It was beyond just clowning around. No one in a presidential debate deliberately and repeatedly contorts their face or does things with their eyes and tongue to look like a frog.

But he did. Because he was sending them the signal that he's one with their lord and savior, Pepe/Kek. While the rest of us were just wondering why he was making funny faces, his cult followers were seeing their god revealed to them.

Yes, Trump has clearly been told about this troll army of his, and he thinks it's pretty cool. He won't get rid of his Twitter account because, as he said on "60 Minutes," with it he was "so much power." He insists that Russia isn't responsible for hacking into the Clinton campaign's computers, and that's because (although he doesn't say this) he believes it's his own troll army that did it.

But he can't resist bragging, even though he can't outright admit his involvement. He tells us that he knows a lot about hacking, and also that he knows things that others don't. This ought to implicate him.

And then the famously ridiculous comment that perhaps the hacking was done by a 400-pound couch potato. Maybe he had been told something about the psychological profile of a typical member of his troll army, and he just couldn't keep from letting it slip that he has nothing but contempt for these people, even though he depends upon them for his political existence.

He knows they'll do his dirty work. Right there in the open, at a debate, he threatens Megyn Kelly after she asks a question he doesn't like. He says he'll "unleash" his "beautiful Twitter account" on her. What does that mean? Do other people talk about their Twitter account like that?

Steve Bannon knows that these internet platforms and the people on them have been weaponized, and that he has been one of the agents of this. Upon being let go by Trump, he lets it be known that this is "#WAR," and that he is going back to Breitbart, his "killing machine."

Trolls are psychopathic sadists, according to psychologists. Those who organize these sick people against political enemies are playing with fire.

And they are waging cyber warfare.

Other aspects of the Russian cyber warfare campaign that influenced our election are being looked at—their hacking into the Hillary Clinton campaign's e-mails, gaining access to the voter rolls and targeting certain voters with certain types of advertising, creating fake news stories, perhaps tampering with the electronic poll books or voting machines or tallies, even the stalking actions of the armies of these internet trolls...but I haven't yet heard anyone discuss the deliberate creation of an online cult to brainwash our young people.

We've heard a lot about the Russian paid internet trolls, and the "bots" that are computer generated, not even real people. But those don't constitute the entire troll army, otherwise there would be no need to brainwash people with these phony coincidences, no need for a pseudo-religious cult to ensure slavish devotion to a cause.

So could we talk about this phenomenon where there is the deliberate creation of an online cult both by a foreign government and by people within our own country actively aiding and abetting it, aimed at brainwashing our young people, that influenced our election?

Because I'm not buying the idea that all of these internet trolls independently just morphed into a pro-Trump internet army. As with the many different white nationalist groups around the world working together for the Eurasian cause, things that at first seem random may not actually be so.

Steve Bannon was supposedly the one, according to the recent book <u>Devil's Bargain</u>, by Joshua Green, who came up with the idea of making use of the "monster power" of the white male online gamer community. He certainly did make use of them, and continues to do so. But he couldn't have put this whole thing together all by himself. This is an advanced combination of cyber and psychological warfare that would require the guidance and assistance of others far more powerful than he to pull it off.

To deliberately create an online cult (and would Bannon even think of that?) would be quite difficult. You'd need psychological experts to decide how best to mess with people's minds, and guide the process along. You'd have to manage to get control of specific online forums. You'd need to stack them with your people and your bots, to make sure that any real users of those sites would get the impression that everyone around them feels a certain way about certain things, to apply peer pressure on them to feel that way, too. You'd need to plant the idea that certain numerological occurrences really mean something, and that users should look for them— then make sure they occur.

You'd have to either manufacture "coincidences," or highlight genuine coincidences that occurred. Or both. It would take advanced computer programs to come up with some of these coincidences. Some of the fake coincidences might even involve murder—predict that someone will die, and then make sure that it happens. I saw an episode of "Law and Order: Criminal Intent" (great show!) where a phony psychic did that. Seemed pretty far-fetched to me. But not as far-fetched as the idea that Trump is an Egyptian god.

And if you're a powerful country like Russia, you might even be able to exert some limited control over the weather in some particular situation, if it helped accomplish the desired result.

I forgot to mention that Pepe/Kek has his own country. Kekistan. Sounds like a country you'd find somewhere in the vicinity of Russia, wouldn't you say? With its own flag. Kind of like the Eurasian flag, and therefore kind of like a swastika. It has a circle containing the design of four "K's," each one facing a different direction, surrounding a central "E." The multiplicity of "K's" could lead one to think it's a KKK flag, especially since that flag and the KKK can be found at many of the same places. The Kekkies find it hugely amusing when people confuse the two. Because the KKK, violence, racism, and people's feelings are all a joke to them. So is it the flag's KKK-ness or its similarity to a swastika that's more unsettling? Or maybe the green color scheme in honor of Lord Pepe/Kek, reflective of the cult's frog-like cold-blooded nature? Hard to say. But if you see it, it's likely to creep you out.

One more meme to report on: God-Emperor Trump. Yes, I know, the gamers and trolls don't really believe that Trump is a god-emperor, just like they don't believe in his divinity through Lords Pepe and Kek. It's just a meme, right.

Through the gamer world, Steve Bannon and more directly, an editor he hired for Breitbart News by the name of Milo Yiannopoulis came up with the idea from a character in the Warhammer 40k role-playing game. This God-Emperor character really isn't a very nice guy—he's responsible for billions of deaths, actually. But since when do trolls care about boring things like ethics or morality? And "God-Emperor" has a nice ring, don't you think? So they created the meme, and Yiannopoulos even publicly referred to "God-Emperor Trump," as if that were a normal kind of way to speak about the president of the United States. Not as much as Pepe maybe, but the meme and the term caught on. Anglin of The

Daily Stormer used it right after Trump was elected, saying, "Our Glorious Leader has ascended to God Emperor." So a neo-Nazi organizer and the editor of a "news" site run by one of the president's advisers agree that Trump is a God Emperor.

Incidentally, Yiannopoulos, as a gay man, has sadly faced some discrimination in the alt-right ethno-fascist community. Not quite as warm and friendly a crowd as you'd think. Similarly, those in the Asian Aryanism movement have found it difficult to gain acceptance from the neo-Nazis for their cause of joining "two great races" to scapegoat the "darker races." Prominent alt-right women are told by alt-right male chauvinists not to be so prominent as they advocate for those who don't think women should have the right to vote. Go figure.

To the list of those who are in on the deification-of-Trump thing, let us add the Republican National Committee (RNC), who on Christmas of 2016 issued a statement with this line: "Just as the three wise men did on that night, this Christmas heralds a time to celebrate the good news of a new King."

So would that be the God-Emperor Trump? Or perhaps Lord Pepe/Kek? Because it certainly wasn't Jesus. Jesus isn't a "new King."

The RNC Spokesman and incoming Press Secretary Sean Spicer's attempted clarification didn't really clear anything up, either, although most people might not have noticed that. Spicer said, "Christ is the King in the Christian faith." Well, yeah. But isn't it odd that Spicer didn't say that they were talking about the Christian faith? Could be faith in Lord Pepe/Kek, or God-Emperor Trump. At least the GOP, not always known for religious tolerance, is welcoming all kinds here. The Left typically looks at evangelical churches for any streaks of religious weirdness in the Republican Party. Thanks to the alt-right, and its Eurasian cyber warriors, we can now include artificially-created internet cults among the usual suspects. —Oh, and maybe parts of the neo-pagan community, such as some of those worshiping the Norse god Odin, a.k.a. Wotan (an acronym for "Will of the Aryan Nation")...

Right now, Trump is the one anointed by Pepe/Kek. But tomorrow it could be somebody else. Or there could be a different artificially-created internet god, with different coincidences and a different meme.   Who knows what this god would demand of its followers? The ones with the ability to create these cults are the ones pulling the strings.

I realize that all this frog stuff may sound absurd, because it is absurd. But ask yourself, why are they doing it? Because so many powerful people wouldn't be doing something just on a whim. Pepe the Frog is a means of mind-control. (And you thought Hillary Clinton was over-the-top in her reaction!)

Minds being controlled by the Eurasianists.

Now, the Eurasianist threat has been reported about in some articles and publications, but certainly not enough to be widely known about.

Some of the journalists and news organizations are already in the tank for Eurasianism. Anyone who tells you that Russia is our friend, or at the very least, isn't really something that we need to worry about, is not to be trusted. For some, it may be that they genuinely see that as the better, more virtuous side. For others, I'd bet it's about money and opportunism. The Eurasianist horse is the one they think will win the race, and they think they'll win big by betting on it. Isn't it odd that someone like radio talk show host Sean Hannity, who could expound upon the principles of conservative philosophy year in and year out, would become one of the main cheerleaders of Donald Trump, who is largely clueless about or antagonistic towards those principles?

This isn't a left/right thing, since the populist elements of both are being manipulated by Russia. What seems like populism may really be intended to serve the Russian oligarchs.

Glenn Beck, interestingly, is one anti-globalist populist type who has been sounding the alarm about some of this. He warned years ago that China and some other countries were quietly getting rid of their U.S. dollars and switching to some other currency, and that that ought to concern us. He also was among the first to go public with talking about Richard Spencer and the alt-right and how that movement of racist extremists was being enabled by Steve Bannon, one of Trump's main men. I was glad that Anderson Cooper has given Beck airtime on his CNN show to discuss the alt-right. A brave move by Cooper, too, considering many people (unfairly, I think) see Beck as a kook.

Maybe there's a fear that it would sound paranoid, like the Red Scare, or overly alarmist. And why get people all worked-up about something unnecessarily?

Maybe it's too slow-moving of a threat to make national news, so it just doesn't.

Or maybe the globalists feel they'd be forced to reveal more about their own world-government agenda than they really want to. No, they're not saints, but they're infinitely more trustworthy than the chaos-fomenting, Aryan-loving Eurasianists. The globalist vision of a world government doesn't erase nations or local governments, it just provides a layer on top of those just as our national government is a layer on top of our state governments. And we are the better for that.

Maybe some people are worried that sounding the alarm about Eurasianism could even sound racist, like anti-Asian. In truth, not all Asian countries are sold on Eurasianism, and some are quite terrified of it. So being a Eurasianist is not the same as being a friend to the people of either Europe or Asia—quite the opposite, I'd say.

I don't know why we're not hearing more about this. But the threat is real.

Hillary Clinton was partly right, years ago, when she talked about a "vast right-wing conspiracy." It's a vast anti-globalist—and therefore anti-American—conspiracy. She and her husband, nothing if not globalists, have been relentlessly targeted.

I'm not a fan of illegal immigration, but people sneaking in from Mexico sure aren't the biggest threat we face. Nor are terrorists of the Islamic extremist variety, despicable as they may be. But there are those who are doing their best to make us see those as the biggest threats to our national security.

Meanwhile, the Eurasianists are already waging war against us. They deceptively appear disorganized, like people who want simply to remain unmolested within their own borders. Meanwhile, they plot to take over the world. The enemy have penetrated our walls and are within our gates. They are weaponizing young people to be disturbed, soulless internet trolls in their army. They have tampered in our election process, to what degree we have yet to determine. In all of this, they have cooperation from the man who is now President of the United States himself, and from those around him. The Eurasianists are acting on their plans for a world domination scheme of the most hideous kind. All from behind the smile of a cartoon frog.

Sources:

Devil's Bargain, by Joshua Green, PenguinRandomHouse.com

Harper's Sept. 2017: "Women of the Alt-Right," by Seyward Darby

"The Rachel Maddow Show," MSNBC

The Palmer Report, palmerreport.com

https://bullshit.ist/meme-magic-is-real-you-guys-16a497fc45b3

http://bigthink.com/paul-ratner/the-dangerous-philosopher-behind-putins-strategy-to-grow-russian-power-at-americas-expense

http://neweasterneurope.eu/articles-and-commentary/1797-eurasian-union-vs-fascist-eurasia

https://www.geopolitica.ru/en/article/ideological-platform-eurasian-movement

http://arctogaia.com/public/eng/Manifesto.html

https://medium.com/@michelledione/the-influential-power-of-memetics-625052287062

http://www.thedailybeast.com/how-breitbart-unleashes-hate-mobs-to-threaten-dox-and-troll-trump-critics

https://www.washingtonpost.com/news/the-intersect/wp/2016/11/09/we-actually-elected-a-meme-as-president-how-4chan-celebrated-trumps-victory/?utm_term=.c3d694bf1755

http://www.independent.co.uk/news/media/online/twitter-is-a-weapon-in-cyber-warfare-1900535.html

http://time.com/4783932/inside-russia-social-media-war-america/

http://www.starktruthradio.com/?p=2245

https://epeak.info/2017/02/10/eurasianism-is-the-new-fascism-understanding-and-confronting-russia/

https://www.cnbc.com/2016/11/23/chinese-officials-are-licking-their-lips-at-trumps-trade-pledge-ian-bremmer.html?view=story&%24DEVICE%24=native-android-mobile

http://www.slate.com/blogs/the_slatest/2017/08/14/donald_trump_s_ties_to_alt_right_white_supremacists_are_extensive.html

https://geopolitics.co/2016/06/23/the-unstoppable-breakneck-speed-expansion-of-the-great-eurasian-corridor/

http://eurasia.com.ru/eurasist_vision.html

http://www.4pt.su/en/content/eurasist-vision

http://www.korea.net/NewsFocus/policies/view?articleId=127627

http://arctogaia.com/public/eng/Manifesto.html

https://qz.com/871975/aleksandr-dugin-putins-favorite-philosopher-is-a-big-fan-of-donald-trump/

http://www.rawstory.com/2017/03/how-an-ancient-egyptian-god-spurred-the-rise-of-trump/

https://www.vox.com/culture/2016/12/30/13572256/2016-trump-culture-war-alt-right-meme

http://www.atimes.com/loss-petrodollar-domination-beginning-form/

http://www.huffingtonpost.com/michael-t-klare/donald-trump-is-giving-the-phrase_b_14745820.html

http://www.alternet.org/comments/news-amp-politics/donald-trump-america-third

https://qrius.com/trump-isolationism-multipolar/

http://bigthink.com/paul-ratner/the-dangerous-philosopher-behind-putins-strategy-to-grow-russian-power-at-americas-expense

https://www.nytimes.com/2017/07/18/books/review/devils-bargain-steve-bannon-donald-trump-joshua-green.html

http://www.redicecreations.com/specialreports/2005/11nov/secreteurasia.html

https://www.counterpunch.org/2016/02/10/dugins-occult-fascism-and-the-hijacking-of-left-anti-imperialism-and-muslim-anti-salafism/

http://www.renegadetribune.com/order-chaos-magic-dark-roots-alt-right/

http://www.nationalreview.com/article/380614/dugins-evil-theology-robert-zubrin

https://qz.com/983460/obor-an-extremely-simple-guide-to-understanding-chinas-one-belt-one-road-forum-for-its-new-silk-road/

http://newparadigm.schillerinstitute.com/our-campaign/build-the-world-land-bridge/

https://larouchepac.com/world-landbridge

http://www.globalresearch.ca/the-brics-the-eurasian-economic-union-eeu-and-the-shanghai-cooperation-organization-sco-towards-a-new-global-financial-architecture/5413714

http://uic.org/com/uic-e-news/458/article/eurasia-friendship-express-2015?page=iframe_enews

http://www.zerohedge.com/news/2016-10-11/eurasian-century-now-unstoppable

https://www.youtube.com/watch?v=9rh1dhur4al

http://metro.co.uk/2017/01/27/neo-nazi-richard-spencer-got-punched-in-the-face-again-6409291/

https://www.vanityfair.com/news/2016/09/donald-trump-jr-pepe-nazi-instagram

https://www.reddit.com/r/The_Donald/comments/5ydnib/mrw_rthe_donald_beat_the_cia_in_the_great_meme/

https://www.psychologytoday.com/blog/your-online-secrets/201409/internet-trolls-are-narcissists-psychopaths-and-sadists

http://www.sciencedirect.com/science/article/pii/S0191886914000324

http://alphavilleherald.com/2016/09/interview-with-alt-right-pepemancer-and-kektrump-supporter-weev.html

http://www.weeklystandard.com/putins-rasputin-endorses-trump/article/2001344

https://www.buzzfeed.com/lesterfeder/this-is-how-steve-bannon-sees-the-entire-world?utm_term=.jfgGXXyyL#.it2GVVxx0

http://russia-insider.com/en/bannon/ri19634

https://winterings.net/2016/11/18/bannon-on-dugin-and-evola/

http://www.nationalreview.com/article/380614/dugins-evil-theology-robert-zubrin

http://crookedtimber.org/2015/03/10/who-is-aleksandr-dugin/

https://www.thenewamerican.com/reviews/books/item/19427-a-review-of-dugin-s-the-fourth-political-theory

https://openrevolt.info/2013/05/19/alexander-dugin-on-white-nationalism-and-other-potential-allies-in-the-global-revolution/

https://www.foreignaffairs.com/articles/2017-07-10/globalism-and-nationalism

https://www.splcenter.org/hatewatch/2017/07/05/daily-stormer-troll-army-threatens-cnn-staffers-over-reddit-user-behind-trumpcnn-gif

http://www.thedailybeast.com/neo-nazi-sued-for-unleashing-troll-army-on-richard-spencers-enemy

https://www.nytimes.com/2016/05/31/world/europe/russia-finland-nato-trolls.html?mcubz=0

https://www.splcenter.org/fighting-hate/extremist-files/individual/andrew-anglin

www.ingramcontent.com/pod-product-compliance
Lightning Source LLC
Chambersburg PA
CBHW050801240726
48654CB00008B/579